The Dance of the Seven Veals

Without the help of the following people this book would have been about as exciting as a fight over the last chunk of liver in the world.

Melinda, Michael, Kay and Nancy at Recycled Paper for digging most of the cartoons out of their efficient filing archives, T. Sirrell for our weekly rap sessions, Di and M.C. for just being friends, Ralph, Kathy, Butch and LeAnne for the times away from work. Dave DeCaro for his patience, wisdom and uncanny knowledge of show tunes, oh, as well as designing the book, The Schicks at A-1 Printing for the many hours they suffered producing the pages, as well as Maria Conchita Garcia who really got the ball rolling in the beginning.

A special thanks to all of my family and relatives who really have no concept of what I do for a living, and who really "don't get" my cartoons; Grandma Mable, Mom and Dad the travelers, Rena (the Elvis inspirator) and Dick "I'm retired" Alphon, Cindy, Nick and Andrew, Kurt the Afrikaner, Mr. Softball Keith, Pam and John from the other side of the family, Veronica from Antigua, Bonnie and Cory, Joshua, Little John and Jared the eating machine.

The Dance of the Seven Veals

by Kevin Pope

St. Martin's Press
New York

Library of Congress Cataloging-in-Publication Data

Pope, Kevin,
   The dance of the seven veals, and other cartoons / Kevin Pope.
     p.   cm.
   ISBN 0-312-05828-4
   1. American wit and humor, Pictorial.   I. Title.
NC1429.P645A4   1991
741.5'973—dc20
                                                  90-28431
                                                    CIP

First Edition: August 1991
10 9 8 7 6 5 4 3 2 1

What cows do on their vacations.

Mommy Deerest.

Learning to dance like James Brown,
the Arthur Murray Way.

Sun Spots.

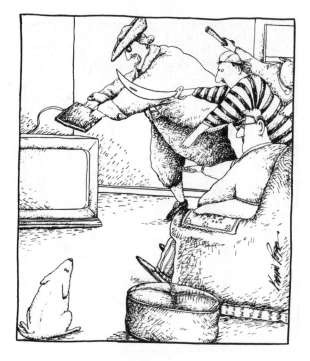

Cable Piracy.

The reluctant stunt dog is finally persuaded.

When Larry reached for his morning newspaper
he found himself suddenly zapped into a parallel universe
where, to his horror, "everything was Gidget!"

The Taft-Hartley Act.

Juggling simplified.

Who's *not* the scourge of the high seas?

Absolutely living too close to the microwave tower.

Yugo, Son of Christine.

A super hard connect the dots game.

Star Truck.

Endangered species.

Pre-debate niceties are exchanged between
Sen. Paul R. Thompson and the
lame-duck candidate, Quacky.

Our new eight-day week.

A ten gallon hat, on a five gallon head.

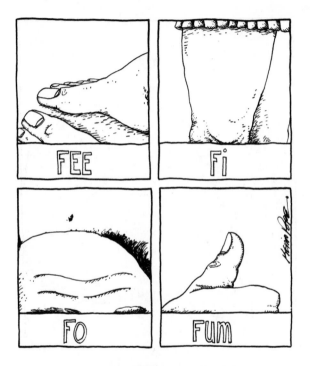

Parts of a giant.

Men from Southern Mars.

Quick as a wink Mike and Spike's place looked like Pompeii as their lava lamp burst out of control.

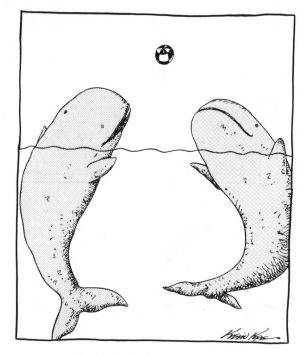

Having just a human of a time.

Hmmm, the bends, Ted thought.
Surely he hadn't forgotten to tell Talbot
about the bends...

Earl and Skeeter rounding up the cows.

Early sidewalk vendors.

Gavin S. Simpson, Boy Scout, Guy about town,
and the lead actor in the all new white production of
"Porgy and Bess."

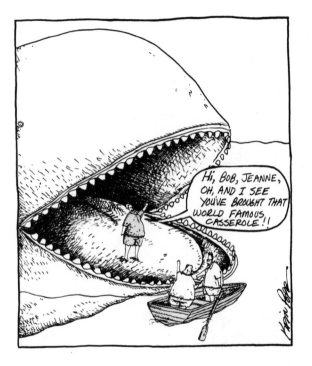

Jonah having a few friends over.

Another black hole starts to form,
and wouldn't you know it, right in Sid's room.

Attack of the Killer B's.

No one, I mean no one, baked bagels
the way Aunt Bernice baked bagels.

Slice of Americana.

After being robbed at gunpoint, Picasso tries to
provide the police with a sketch of the suspect.

Elwood quickly found out that the light
at the end of the tunnel was a train.

The boy with the big fantastic head.

Voice of America (Hollywood, Calif.).

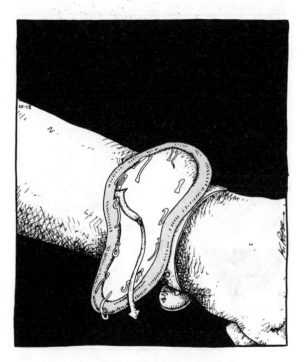

The Salvador Dali wristwatch.

Using his lariat, Festus teaches ol' Sparky
how to read and write.

Helen of Troy, the face that launched
a thousand ships.

In 1961, Wanda threw away all of her toys,
but now they're back...and they want some answers.

Hogan's Heroes.

Dooley looked like just another wimp, but he had that darn force field.

The Vulcan and the snowman.

The last thing Romanus said at Pompeii.

Nature lessons with Tippy.

WICKED WITCH
OF THE SOUTH

WICKED WITCH
OF THE NORTH

MY THIRD GRADE
TEACHER

WICKED WITCH
OF THE WEST

Wicked Witches illustrated.

Aerial stampede.

Things that don't improve our standard of living.

Everyone knew that the fun was just about to end
once the Sponge Boy showed up.

Heidi turns 90.

The Life and Times of Judge Roy's Bean.

Martha was going stark-raving mad.
Not only had her mood ring been stuck on red for the
past two weeks, but her finger had swollen and
she couldn't get the ring off.

Things that could be out there.

The sky's the limit.

The puppies, lost in the jungle and raised by giraffes,
finally find their way back home.

The problems with desert shopping.

Mongolia enters the space race.

For years, early sailors had to rely on
the stars as their maps.

Rhino-ka-bobs.

Moses, as a kid, tries to take a swim.

Ted and Leona, the suburban limbo gods.

Cat nip.

Male baldness patterns illustrated.

Cat on a hot tin roof.

Another important crossroad along the
evolutionary trail.

Arnold F. Schwartz, chairman of the board.

Whoops, Noah leaves a bit early.

Chet sure liked his barbieques.

An early quest for fire…milk, and a loaf of bread.

Cowards.

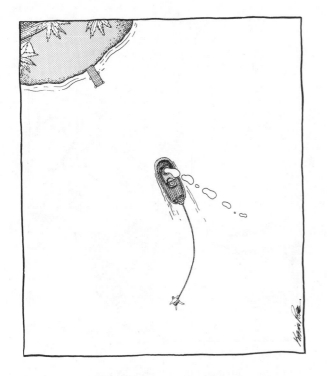

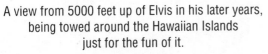

A view from 5000 feet up of Elvis in his later years,
being towed around the Hawaiian Islands
just for the fun of it.

The Pharaoh Godmother.

Jacob trying to paint his house with the new ladder he invented.

Attack of the left-handed people.

Ginny soon realized why she was being chased...
it was after Labor Day, and she was still
wearing those white shoes.

Vincent Van A-go-go.

Earl's try at sports.

Santa meets up with his evil twin brother Santú
on his way to the reindeer stables.

Oh, oh…alleygators.

Moses turned the water into blood, day into night,
and leftovers into just lovely pot-luck casseroles.

Ed and Chuck, out witch-hunting.

Ensign Kangaroo

Chief Petty Officer

Brigade Commander

Captain Kangaroo

The complete military history of Captain Kangaroo.

Nick "Windy" Matzo was found guilty by Association.

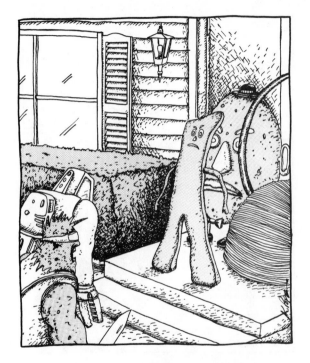

Not wanting their reunion party ruined, the toys from the '60s stand their ground against those gate-crashing toys from the '80s.

Lifestyles of the Poor and Unknown.

Tails from the dark side.

Bum steer.

English Royalty's emotions illustrated:
A. Not having any fun.
B. Having absolutely too much fun.

Moscows.

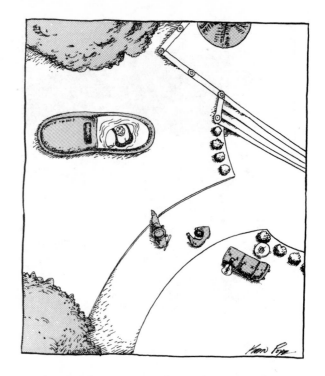

A view from 500 feet up of Elvis and a Graceland
Security Guard flipping a coin to see who gets to wrestle
a devoted fan out of his Blue Suede Shoe Birdbath.

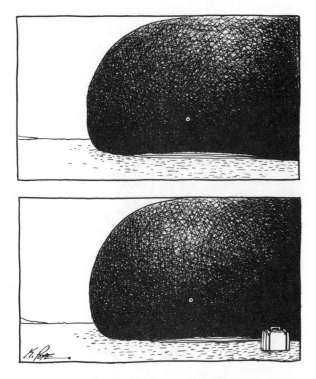

The difference between a beached whale,
and a vacationing one.

Smedley makes a mistake.

Dampened spirits.

Sparky, the semi-talkative dog.

The fashion fad for this spring is marine life.

Spam, the world's most misunderstood meat.

The difficult seven-ten split rarely used by
the big game hunters.

The Soul Train celebrity scramble board,
or just a cruel hoax?

First recorded naval battle victory.

Lester, in hog heaven.

Ronald knew that he'd be in for quite a tussle
tonight,…the beanbag chair was still up, and yep,
it had been drinking again.

Greta at first was terrified as she flushed the dustball
out from under the bed, but as soon as it swooped up
the family dog, she became mad...vacuuming mad.

Cows from around the world.

Texas, the Lone Star state.

"Bear essentials."

Chess for morons.

Spot, near the brink of disaster.

Stu and Monty watch as the herd of cows
fly south for the winter.

With uncanny swiftness the defense suffered a
serious blow as a new surprise witness
waddled toward the stand.

The new Kitty-Selector, and how it works.

Visitors from outer space.

The Tunisian orchestral string section.

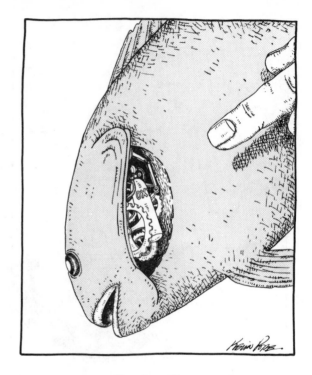

How fish gills work.

Wallabies.

Gravity wins again.

Yes, even the cows felt gripped by the Wave Fever.

Europe on 50 cents a day.

Art's first indication that his mouthwash
just isn't cutting it.

The Supremes Court.

The Sixth Annual Greater Nevada Air Show.

The Rockettes of Gibraltar.

Stupid animal sounds.

Mickeyroni.

Accidentally walking into his parents bedroom,
Little Timmy is quickly subjected to
"Health Class, the Home Version."

Ed was speechless. The cat had his tongue, and he wondered how he was going to ask for it back.

GHOSTS

ALIENS

MONSTERS

Haircuts like this

Real scary things.

Medusa goes through a new beautician
almost every week.

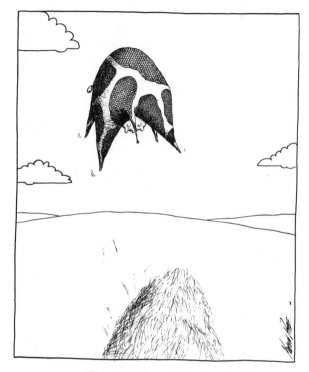

"The needle *was* in the haystack."

Vern would soon find out that he was up against the best hide-and-seek player in the world.

Caveguys.

Kitty litter.

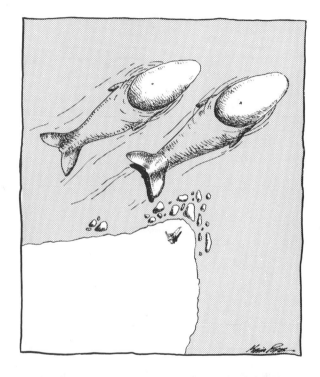

A view from 3000 feet up of Elvis sending off a couple of Grey whales with an absolutely beautiful medley of his Gospel hits in a way that only the king could.

This is exactly what happens when
elephants don't floss.

The man who saw tomorrow.

Alphabet soup from around the world.

Giraffiti.

Margaret Doody, Tuttle, North Dakota,
still waiting for her ship to come in.

When the pasture becomes real boring,
cows become creative.

Guido's new Catillac.

Another pork by-product.

Al in Wonderland.

Sitting Bull.

The oink blot test.

Boy, those shots were sure close, Ed thought.
And hey, by the way, where did his practical joking
friends run off to?

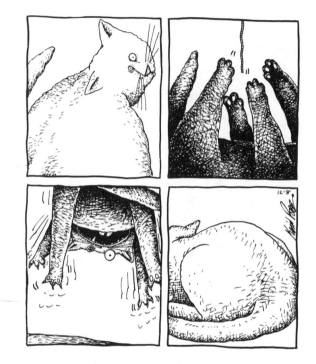

Guess which kitty found out where the catnip was kept?

Wally the Duck Boy's plan to run away to join the circus
was carefully thought out to the very last detail,
or so he thought.

Gus liked puppies, but gosh, they hadn't made
a peep all day.

Levitation as a hobby.

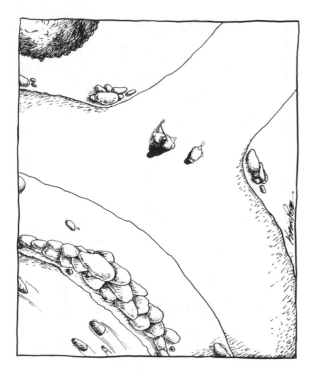

A view from 1500 feet up of the King of Rock and Roll and his duck Waddles discussing diet hints and the history of Polyester Jumpsuits.

In hopes of bettering herself, her way of life, her self esteem, Alice, with a deep breath, walks right out of Ted's life and directly into...

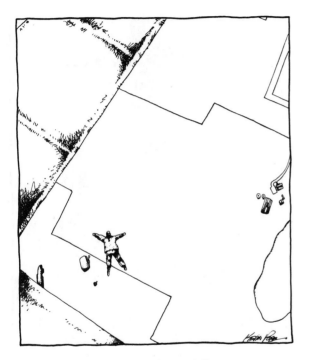

Nonstop to Kokomo daily.

DaVinci goofing around.

A well deserved iron curtain call for Boris and Binky.

A really proud pig farmer, dammit.

On Valentine's Day in Albania, the village women affectionately pummel their lovers repeatedly with a sturdy stick,...much to the man's delight.

How to teach your cat to swim.

Flamingo dancers.

May 5th, 1957, Bud's brain shriveled up and slipped out of his ear, never to be heard from again.

In a state of shock.

Ted knew it was a big, big world out there, but it really
didn't matter to him...he had a big, big hat.

Moscows on the Hudson

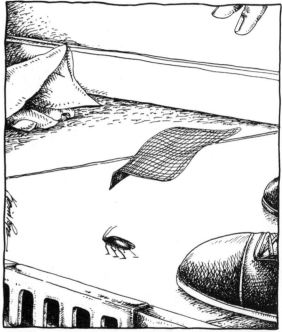

Following Marlon's expert instructions, Jim is quickly able to net and finally wrestle to the ground a fine example of the Big Apple's wildlife in another exciting adventure of Mutual of New York City's Wild Kingdom.

The art of exterior decorating.

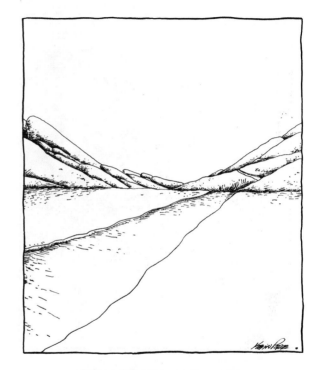

Burma, Monday morning rush hour.

Oh, just great…after a terrible day at work,
the last thing Fred wanted to do was to have to
round up the kids' science projects again.

Teddy Roosevelt and the rough riders.

Oh, oh…Harold forgot to pay
this month's gravity bill again.

FaLL

Winter

Spring

Summer

Jed Clampett's line of women's shoes.

Summer fun in Siberia.

Earl had a terrible day at work, and now all he needed was to have those darn, big scary invisible animals show up on his way home.

ON THE AVERAGE, GLACIERS MOVE TWO FEET A YEAR.

ON THE AVERAGE.

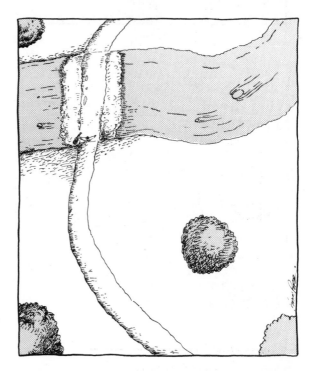

A view from 3000 feet up of Elvis demonstrating his new super powers since he was declared the King of Rock and Roll.

At first, Scotty thought that keeping a pet whale would be fun...that, of course, was before he found out the dang thing ate four tons of plankton a day.

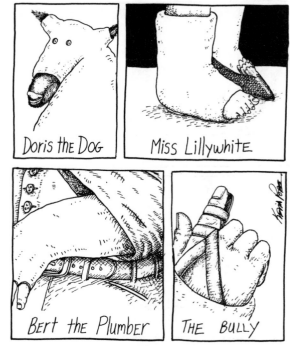

Doris the Dog

Miss Lillywhite

Bert the Plumber

THE BULLY

Cast of Characters.

Aliens finally find intelligent life on Earth.

The Deuces are wild.

A house with a lot of closet space.

The Dance of the Seven Veals.

It was useless. No matter how hard he tried to use the Vulcan mind melt, Spock just couldn't get through to these creatures.

LAND HO HO, HO!!

Santa the Sailor Man.

It was a hot summer day, and the city was ripe with
the typical smelly stench of August afternoons.
Needless to say, folks weren't real happy to see Fat
Freddie walking around without a shirt on.

Fer away

Yonder

Purty near

Over Thar

Inglish lesson #3 – distances.

Where old jokes go.

Once again, another average American citizen is
wickedly tricked by the sewer boogyman.

"Mike and Spike locate the dense jungle
of the Antarctica."

When Sleestax moves into the neighborhood.

Cowbells.

A dog eat dog world.

Morris code.

When someone slipped a Mickey into Ned's drink,
he quickly countered with a Donald.

Much to Leona's surprise, the plot had thickened again.

Stuff that dreams are made of.

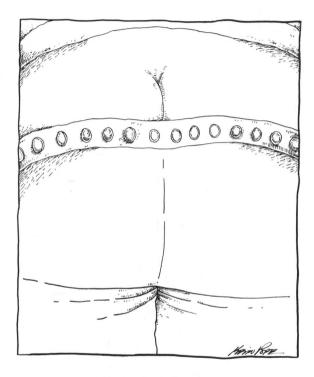

Elvis touching his toes.

Fried Chicken.

What people without hobbies do in their spare time.

One day, lima beans learned to talk.

Someone's been into the cookies again, and...
hey, all of the helium is gone too.

Good and bad duck decoys.

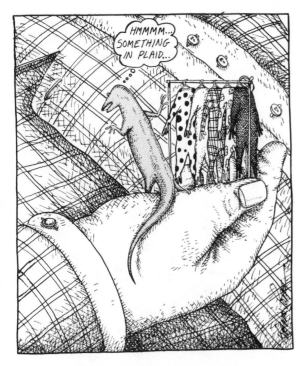

How chameleons change colors.

Doris hates that time of the month when her body chemistry changes, her muscles ache, her feet swell up and her weight shifts to that of helium.

Single cell division.

Cletus Wayne for, "Why you should never try to feed a grizzly with only half a sandwich."

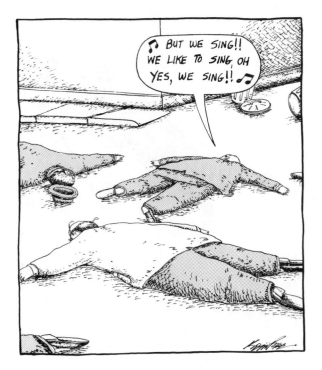

Dead men tell no stories.

Hey, Nick wasn't the smartest guy, but shit like this really baffled the hell out of him.

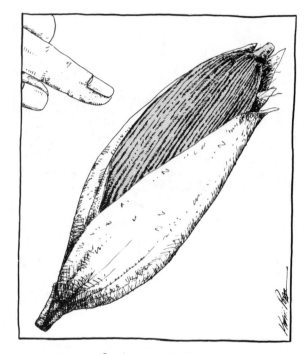

Corduroy on the Cob.

Leonard and Sylvia, 20th century cliff dwellers.

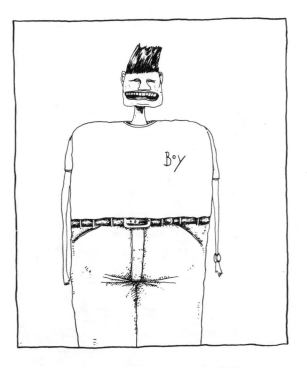

According to The Boy, you've got to
live life on the edge...
or thereabouts.

A counter attack.

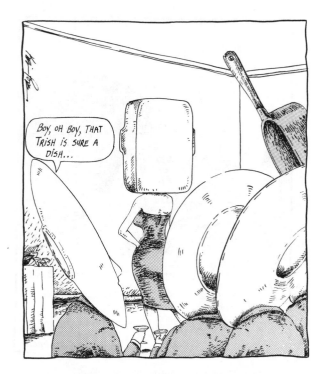

Whenever the platehead boys got together,
hormone levels were sure to flare up.

Today's hunter-gatherers.

Elvis appears in front of Earl, and quickly
warns him before he had ordered.

The Amityville garage sale.

Goober peas.

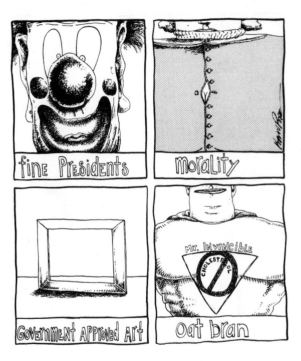

Thanking the decade of the 80's for giving us,...

Walt knew that it just wasn't every day that a guy
gets to rub elbows with a celebrity, let alone
an all-time great one like Hopsing of Bonanza.

"Top Dog."

Little Bo Diddley

Fred gets a visit from the Happy Reaper.

Phantom of the Oprah.

Stan knew this was the archeological find of the '80s!
The ceremonial burial ground of the
once beloved Earth shoe.

Why Little Johnny can't read.

The sinking of the Titanic; the raising of the Titanic;
and the Titanic as Esther Williams.

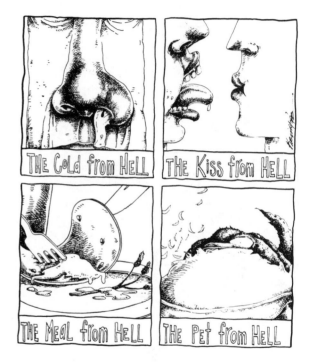

THE Cold from Hell

THE Kiss from Hell

THE Meal from Hell

THE Pet from Hell

Stuff from Hell.

Ernie was never again afraid of those
neighborhood thugs, once his newest invention,
bulletproof Jello had been perfected.

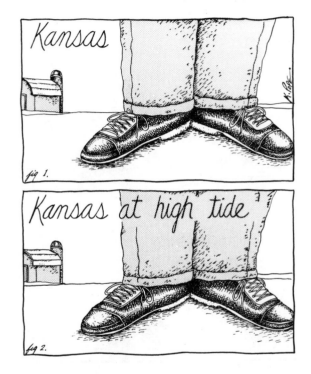

Ollie, Ollie, all in freeeee!!!

Santas from around the World.

Jack Lord.

Some assembly required.

Teddy Roosevelt's first bear hunt.

Little Lizzie Borden does some
after-Christmas shopping.

"Panic in the desert."

It was the worst that could happen...being shipwrecked
on a deserted island with just a black and white TV.

The Lawn Ranger.

Francis and Puff, near the Arctic circle.

In a glass of Milk

as a topping

In a Jello dish

with your cereal

Four ways to make Spam even more delicious.

Author Stuff

Kevin and his wife Kim, their two children Griffith and Justin, their dog Cleo the Dog, their cat Domino, and the toad between the rocks, live in Bloomington, Indiana, which is just a stone's throw away from the rest of the world.